SOLVING
the RIDDLE
of SELF

Solving *the* Riddle *of* Self

The Search for Self-Discovery

JOHN POWELL, S.J.

ThomasMore

A DIVISION OF TABOR PUBLISHING

Allen, Texas

Illustrations by Pin Yi Wu

Cover illustration by Ed Leach

Cover design by Dennis Davidson

Send all inquiries to:

Thomas More Publishing
200 East Bethany Drive
Allen, Texas 75002–3804

Printed in the United States of America

ISBN 0–88347–300–3

1 2 3 4 5   99 98 97 96 95

TABLE OF CONTENTS

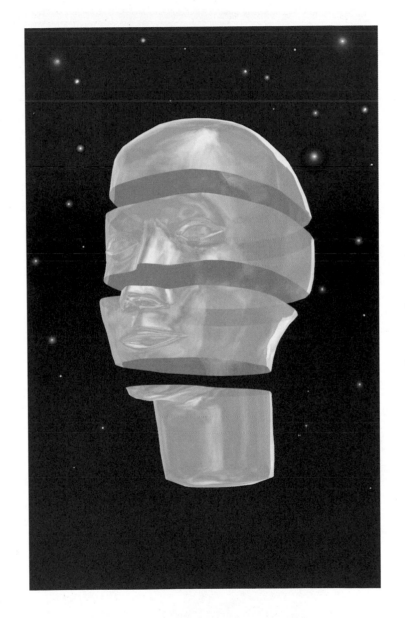

I know myself only partially.

Foreword

In previous books and articles, I have tried to share some of the things that have helped me personally. I have written nothing that was not tried and tested in the laboratory of my own life.

The most recent of my personal "helps" concerns self-knowledge. This seems to be a fact for me. I know myself only partially. Only very slowly am I getting to know my true self. It is at least for me a gradual and lifelong process. Sometimes it is painful. Other times it is joyful. Always it is worthwhile.

I once thought that a book on this topic would be useless. I assumed that if any of us was asked, "Do you really know yourself?" everyone would answer "Yes!" I once believed that people would certainly say, "Of course, I know myself." They might even be a bit puzzled by the very question. I figured that most of us would think, "I mean, if I don't know myself, who does?"

Then I began asking people, "Do you know yourself?" Surprisingly, the answers came back, "Only partly . . . Not very well . . . Somewhat . . . ." So I decided that most of us (including myself) are ready for confrontation with the question: "Who am I really?" We are even ready to admit that sometimes others know us better than we know ourselves. In fact, I sometimes think that the last person that we get to know well is ourselves. For many years I wondered why this is so. If we have really spent so much time with ourselves, why are we such strangers to self-knowledge? Over these years of wonder I have learned much that has been helpful to me.

I decided, therefore, to write this book. My hope is to share with you what I have learned along the way in my own life. The most haunting question over these years of wonder was this: Who am I really? Among the things I think I have learned are the most common problems that block us from self-knowledge. No matter how hard we try to come to know ourselves better, if there are blocks in the way, we will usually make little or no progress. I've also come to recognize and respect the power of the past and the way it affects our present behaviors. Such insight has enabled me to form a theory that has helped me understand myself. I have come to understand something of the patterns in my life. The patterns of behavior were clear in so many examples from my own life and the lives of others who have shared with me.

As we come to know ourselves better, we inevitably find parts of us that are not healthy but rather destructive pieces. So we begin a series of questions about change. Can I actually change? Do I really want to change? How do I go about changing? In trying to answer these questions, we find ourselves dealing with the solution of the problems blocking self-knowledge. Finally, I think I have come upon ways which can incorporate into our lives the practice of growth in self-discovery.

Consequently, this book will be divided into five parts: (1) The Problem, (2) The Theory, (3) Examples, (4) The Solution, and (5) The Practice. I hope that what has been helpful to me will be helpful to you, too.

On now to Part One, The Problem.

*There are various forces
struggling inside us.*

I

The Problem: The Major Blocks to Self-Knowledge

Most of us wonder at times who we really are. It is not a purely up-in-the-air, speculative problem. We actually pause at moments of reflectiveness to wonder what we are doing, and what drives us. Why do we instinctively like certain things, and instinctively avoid other things? Why do certain things turn us "on" and others turn us "off"?

The theory of "transactional analysis" proposes that there are really three parts struggling inside each of us: the parent (the messages we were given as children), the adult (our own minds and wills, thinking our own thoughts and making our own choices) and the child (the storehouse of our feelings and emotional responses). Somehow most of us are not surprised that there are various forces struggling inside us.

Sometimes they bang into one another. Often the result for most of us is confusion. (For a more complete development of the three "ego states" please see my book *The Secret of Staying in Love*, pp. 103–105.)

Sometimes we can clearly see what others are doing, what they are about and what they are "into." But when we turn to look at ourselves, we find all sorts of apparently contradictory evidence. We can only wonder why and ask: Who am I really? What do I really want in my life? Often we know what others have told us to be or to do. But under all these directions, we wonder: Who am I?

THE FAMOUS THREE DEFENSES (BLOCKS)

Sometimes I think that the problem of getting to know ourselves comes from the difficulty we have with digging into the layers of ourselves. As we try to dig through these layers we are often stopped abruptly by what seems like solid granite. The common interpretation of this impasse is that we have all developed defenses which are intended to spare us from honest confrontation with ourselves.

These defenses form shields around us. They are developed to prevent us from being overwhelmed by life. However, these defenses also shield us from knowing our own inner and true selves. Over the years they have become barriers which block us from honest self-discovery.

THE FIRST OF THE MAJOR DEFENSES: REPRESSION

The first of the three most common defenses is called REPRESSION. We are all capable of hiding the truth from ourselves. We repress that truth by pushing it down into our unconscious minds. Whatever we do not want to recognize in ourselves we can simply block from consciousness by repression. One of our leading psychiatrists thinks that in average unreflective persons, 90 percent of what we do, say and think is based on unconscious materials. If you were to ask these persons why they did such and such, they would not know the real reason. However, the good news is that this repressed matter is like wood held under water. Repressed material is always trying to surface for recognition. At times, stress itself can force us to look at these things which at some previous time we preferred to hide.

Psychology tells us that there are three levels of every human mind: (1) the conscious, (2) the subconscious and (3) the unconscious. Our conscious mind is engaged with whatever we are doing and thinking about at any given moment. As you are reading these words, they are in your conscious mind. However, we also have a subconscious mind. We keep on record in our subconscious minds things like the dates of anniversaries and birthdays, the multiplication table and so forth. These are the facts and memories we store for later recall. While this material is not in our conscious minds, we are aware of having filed the matter in the subconscious. It is available for use whenever we want to recall it.

We also have an unconscious mind. There we hide things we don't want to face or to live with. The unconscious has been called the basement of the mind. We are not all aware of either the process of hiding or the material hidden in these basements.

It is important to know this much, that what we have stored in the unconscious is buried alive, not dead. These hidden things (events, feelings, reactions, prejudices) continue to haunt, to bother and to influence us. However, just as we are not aware of the things we have hidden, we are also not aware of their impact on our thoughts, actions and reactions. And this impact can so easily make a great difference in our daily lives.

Let me try a fictitious example. Let us suppose that I resented my own mother. My mother often assured me that she had once gone to death's door to give me life. But my feelings toward her were still negative. I tried to share this resentment with childhood friends. However, they told me in what seemed like scolding terms that I must be an "ingrate." Now I felt not only resentment for my mother, but also shame toward myself for having such a feeling. I simply could not live with this "shameful" feeling. So I drove my resentment down deep into my unconscious. I hid it in the basement of my mind where I would no longer be aware of it. The result of this was that it removed my sense of shame. It was a good defensive move, but it would have many negative results later in my life.

In fact, by what is called "reaction formation," I had come to think of my mother as a "saint." Reaction formation means that this reaction was programmed into me during my formative years. This compensation soon became "overcompensation." So I cherished her person or memory far beyond her reality. This overcompensation of exaggerated admiration kept my buried resentment for her from ever surfacing for recognition.

Since the time of this repression, I was not conscious of any resentment for my mother. However, this resentment was not really dead in me, but very much alive. It continued to exert an influence on me and my behavior. My hidden resentment flared up in all the wrong situations and was directed toward all the wrong people. Most of them were usually women. As I vented my resentment on them, it never occurred to me that my real but disguised resentment was really for my own mother. The fact is that my mother had become the lens through which I looked at all other women.

THE SECOND DEFENSE: RATIONALIZATION

The second defense we commonly use is called RATIONALIZATION. Rationalization usually occurs when we are in the position of choosing between good and evil. At least this is the most common situation in which we use this defense. We can at first dimly recognize the possibility of evil in what we are considering. So, if we wish to choose the evil, we must rationalize that evil until it somehow appears as good. It goes this way. My mind (the power to know) proposes a choice to my will (the power to choose). The will can only choose that which is of personal benefit. It can't choose evil as an evil. It has to be reaching out for something that is seen as good. So my will can and does command my mind. My will orders my mind in this case to rationalize the evil. As the old saying goes: "I have tailored the facts to fit my own choices."

For example, I find your wallet. It contains much money, but it also has your name and address in it, printed out very clearly. I think about all the things I could do with your money. They all sound so "tempting." And the more I dangle that carrot in front of the hungry rabbit of my desires, the more I want it. My power to know—my mind—has proposed a choice to my will: to keep your money or to return it to you. Let us suppose that I choose the immoral good: to keep your money. In this case my will orders my mind to rationalize the matter. I must make what formerly seemed evil appear as good.

So my mind dutifully thinks about taking from the rich and giving to the poor. "You must be the rich and I am the poor." Finally, my rationalization process is completed, and I am . . . Robin Hood, taking from the rich and giving to the poor. We are all capable of this kind of rationalization, of such self-delusion. So most of the time we really need to talk over these private reasonings with another person whose moral compass we can trust.

In the world today, the media, our entertainment and culture do not help us to be honest with ourselves. In fact, they help us rationalize by doing much of the work for us. They make things which at first seem wrong to us sound so right. "How can it be wrong when it feels so right?" Societally we seem to have rationalized violence, sexual indulgence, lying and stealing. We work on our vocabulary first. Rationalization always begins with words. So, with the help of the media and movies, we speak of "wiping people out," or we "off" them. In physical seduction, we "get lucky." Lying is "packaging" or "spinning." Stealing is no longer stealing, you know. After all, this is the age of the great "rip-off." So we speak of a "fast buck" instead of a sleazy deal. Our media has helped us euphemize evil. In our effort to rationalize we cannot afford to be honest, to name things truthfully.

THE THIRD DEFENSE: DENIAL

The third of our defenses is simply called DENIAL. We close our minds to the reality that we don't want to face. We block out a part of reality because it is emotionally painful. One common example is the denial of death. In his Pulitzer Prize-winning book, Ernest Becker says that we all have a "concealed psychosis" about death. We simply have cut off a part of reality. Consequently, we don't open fully either to the sorrows or to the joys of life. We trim down reality to a size that we think we can handle. Harry Stack Sullivan, the psychiatrist of inter-personal relationships, calls this denial "selective inattention." He insists that we pick out a "security operation," something like a specialty, and then simply deny the opposite. It does not fit into the picture we have chosen to see.

For example, if I pick out as my "security operation" being a humorist, I would have to deny all the sadness and cruelty in life. This is my way of viewing life. I simply take the stand that "everything's coming up roses." If anyone tries to dissuade me of this in one way or another, I let them know that my mind is closed. I keep repeating the thesis by which I live. Incidentally, my permanent address is "On the Sunny Side of the Street."

I am told that the average period of denial for an alcoholic is seven years. For seven long years the average alcoholic will sincerely maintain, "I have no problem. I

We rarely argue about the real issues.
We pick out straw men or women
with whom to do battle.

can take it or leave it alone." The family members of the alcoholic person usually feel so disgraced and/or embarrassed that they, too, deny the problem. "Oh, Daddy (or Mommy) drinks, but he (or she) isn't what you would call an alcoholic. There is no real problem." And yet they allow the drinking to upset everybody's life. No problem?

Andy Griffith appeared in a movie (made for TV) called *Under the Influence*, in which he portrays an alcoholic. It is interesting to see how the various members of his family cover over and deny the fact. At the end of the movie, after Andy has literally drunk himself to death, the denying wife is pictured sitting with her family. "I just know," she says, "that Daddy is coming through that door at any minute now." If denial is the name of the human game, it is a sad and cruel game that keeps us living with unreality. I once asked a recovering alcoholic why alcoholics need meetings. She answered, "Because denial tries to reenter your thinking and your life. Meetings help us to continue facing reality; they help us remember how it was."

So it is somehow a lie about ourselves or others that we sincerely tell ourselves. "Oh, no, I am not angry. . . . I am not jealous. . . . My family was just fine, not dysfunctional at all. . . . I rarely make mistakes. . . . My dear mother was a saint. . . . No, I would never lie." We go on blithely believing and mouthing these lies about ourselves and others, while the opposite reality stares at us or boils somewhere deep inside us. Unfortunately, this staring or boiling is all located in the unconscious, out of sight. Our emotions of anger or jealousy can escape only in what are called "displaced emotions."

These unacknowledged emotions are almost always vented on the wrong issue or on the wrong person.

In fact, we rarely argue about the real issues. We pick out straw men or women with whom to do battle. "So, Stupid, how much did you pay for those shoes?" "Well, Harry, are you ever going to fix the screen door you said you would fix five years ago?" When Daddy is pushed around all day by his boss, he finally arrives home. He trips over a roller skate and unleashes a volley of hard sayings. If you or I were to ask him, "Are you really that upset by the roller skate?" he would undoubtedly answer, "Yes! I could have broken my neck on that [censored] thing." Does he really believe this? Yes. Is he really angry about the roller skate? No. He's angry about his job and his boss, but it is so much safer to rage at the kids. So he denies anger for his boss and ventilates it on his kids.

Sad fact: Denial is indeed the name of the game.

THE BEGINNING: THE WAYS OF BECOMING UNREAL

First, let me say that "mask," "act," "role," "strategy," "adaptation," "pretense," and so forth, all refer to the same basic reality. They refer to the way we act and want to come across to ourselves and to others. They imply a denial of who we really are.

I have heard it said that between birth and five years of age, the average child receives 431 negative messages every day. Now a negative message may not be a full-blown scolding, but a simple, "No, that is not the way you tie shoes. . . . Get down from there; you could be hurt. . . . Now be quiet, I've had a hard day. . . . Oh, look,

you've got dirt on your clothes. . . . Go wash your hands.
. . . Play outside so I can get a little rest. . . . Please don't
bang on that piano; you'll give me a headache. . . . Put
that down. . . . You shouldn't do that. . . . Don't even
think about it. . . . Don't touch that! . . . No, you're too
small! . . . You'll ruin your dinner." And so forth, 431
times a day. And since first impressions are the most
lasting, almost all of us develop in these early years king-
sized inferiority complexes. We bring these complexes
into life and retain much of them throughout life. And
so we begin our defense work.

We repress our real feelings because they seem unac-
ceptable to others. We rationalize that to get along or to
survive we must somehow behave in ways that are
acceptable, or at least not disapproved by others. Such
behavior does not contribute to our personal growth. We
reason, however, that these masks will help us get
through life without more negative messages. In making
this adaptation, we deny our real and original selves. For
the approval of our parents or peers we forfeit our own
freedom!

The first step in this process is usually to pick out an
adaptation, a role, a mask of denial. We choose a strategy
that will get us through life with the minimum amount
of further damage to our already dented self-esteem. The
role, adaptation or mask that we pick out usually
depends on our temperament, ability and natural incli-
nations, the birth order in our family, or the way we
think we can get noticed or avoid being noticed. So
some of us became shy, and others outgoing. Some of us
became athletes, while others grew up as intellectuals.
We became "Mommy's little helper" or "Mommy's little

nuisance" depending on how we could get through life and get our needed attention most easily.

One young man whom I taught many years ago was doing very poorly in my course. So I asked him one day, "Are you trying to fail this course?" I was surprised by his quick, "Yes." So I asked, "Why?" He told me with great difficulty how he had been his father's pride and joy until about age ten. Then suddenly his father became too busy (famous) to play games with him, to listen to him recite and so forth. The young man concluded with this: "The only time now that I know my father cares is when he yells at me. And he yells whenever I flunk a course." I believe the title of that song is: "What I Did for Love."

Which of these life-strategies have you played? It's okay if you choose more than one.

The Perfectionist
The Reformer
The Lover
The Caretaker
The Nice Guy
The Artist
The Victim Soul
The Martyr
The Performer
The Success
The Thinker
The Brain
The Loyalist
The Faithful One
The Happy One
The Leader
The Negotiator

The Obedient One
The Reliable One
The Peacemaker
The Humorist
The Athlete
The Pleaser
The Hard-to-Please One
The Troublemaker
Other?

The problem is that denial slowly but surely becomes the name of our game. It becomes a way of life. We have practiced our act so long and so well that it is now very difficult to distinguish our real selves from our pretended selves. Sometimes we may need a gentle nudge from friends who are willing to be honest and objective with us.

There comes to mind a friend whose main aspiration in life was to become an "actor." All his emotions were "up for hire," not genuine. When confronted with this, he explained that he had been entertaining others all his life. He was the designated entertainment at home from age five onward. The role he played out in his family was that of the performer. He once quoted to me that old show biz saying: "Once your learn to fake sincerity, you've got it made."

I also remember a young man who was very jealous about his "girlfriend." He insisted on knowing things like where she had been from 11:30 to 11:45. However, he had this going in his favor: he was a very honest person. He said that his parents were divorced because his father had been untrue to his mother. He told me that his mother had told him of his father's "cheating." I must have asked him on five separate occasions if this had

*Sometimes we think that our mask
really is our true self.*

anything to do with his own jealousy and possessiveness. Finally, after some honest soul-searching, he recognized this as a fact. Denial is the name of the game, and it does not die easily. Denial is also the source of our personal justification. Sometimes we think that our mask really is our true self. "This is the way I am. I was this way in the beginning, am now and shall be forevermore," we say. It is a good way to postpone confrontation with the truth. A good way to avoid change and never grow.

This is briefly part of the problem of acquiring self-knowledge. We take a bruised ego and cover it over with a role or mask. We rehearse this role so long that in the present moment of life we wonder where the role ends and the real self begins. Then we ask ourselves the embarrassing question: Who am I really? The answer is clouded by our own cover-ups. The blocks of repression, rationalization and denial prevent us from getting behind the mask or under the role. We just don't know our true selves.

QUESTIONS FOR REFLECTION

1. What question have you asked about yourself which you could not answer? (Like "Why am I attracted to this person or thing and repelled by this other?")
2. Recall three different events in which one of the three ego states (Parent, Adult, Child) predominated in you. Which of these three ego states habitually dominates you, your thinking and your behavior.
3. What do you think about the psychiatric opinion that ninety percent of what we say,

do, think, feel is based on "unconscious material?"

4. The unconscious mind remains active in us even while we sleep. It furnishes the matter for our dreams. What significance do your dreams seem to have in your life? Are your dreams rewarding or punishing? What do you think this means?

5. What do you think you can do to dredge your own unconscious mind? Would this be valuable?

6. Identify one occasion of rationalization from your own past. How has society (media, entertainment) helped you to rationalize?

7. What is your own "security operation," and your consequent "selective inattention?"

8. Try to recall a period in you life when you denied something that you can now admit to yourself? Have you experienced the use of denial by yourself or others? Do you or some-one you know experience this denial with regard to alcoholism or other addictions?

9. When or with whom do you most often displace your emotions by arguing about the wrong issue?

10. What role was assigned to you, or what mask do you now wear? Do you think of yourself as open and honest ("What you see is what you get!")? Do you tend to see through your own mask?

II

The Theory: Our Past As Prologue

I am told that the human brain weighs about three pounds. Scientists say it is the finest computer ever made. It stores quadrillions of memories and messages. In fact, neurologists estimate that if a computer were ever built to store all the things that the human brain retains, it would be ten stories tall and cover the state of Texas. In fact, everything that has ever happened to you and to me, from our prenatal experiences on, is recorded on these very sensitive and retentive instruments known as our brains.

Of course, we can't retrieve it all as needed. The problem of memory is "recall." Some of the material stored in our brains obviously antedates our active memory, which usually begins about ages three to five. Other materials have been quietly but effectively repressed, rationalized or simply denied out of existence. But all remain indelibly engraved on our brains and influence our actions and reactions.

It is very important to know that it is all this stored material that makes us secure or insecure. It also makes judging the motivation and intention of self or others seem a bit silly. How am I supposed to know what is recorded on another's brain? I don't even know what is stored in my own!

OUR YESTERDAYS LIE HEAVILY UPON OUR TODAYS

Briefly, my own theory is this: What comes from us, in the form of thoughts, feelings or actions, comes out of something that has been stored up in us. If I get angry or envious, there has to be some anger or envy already in me. And, chances are, it has been in me for a very long time. If there is a lot of anger in me, it will squirt out often and in various directions. I'll be like the man with an even temper: always mad about something. But how did whatever is in me get in me in the first place? That question brings me to the second part of my theory.

I feel sure that whatever is in me right now goes way back to other times in my life. It may have been modeled for me. It may be that I have incorporated it as part of my "act." It may be from my interpretation of something that happened or didn't happen to me at some time in my early life. Our past thus becomes the prologue for the

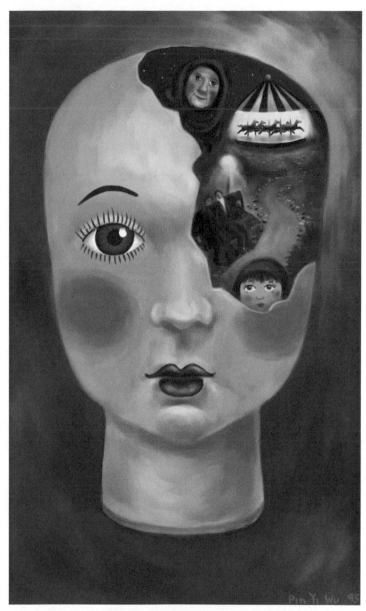

Our past becomes the prologue for the present and future days of our lives.

present and future days of our lives. Sometimes, when I discover something in myself for the first time, I find it difficult to trace it back to one event or one interpretation. This newly discovered habit or mannerism may well be like the roots of a tree spreading out in many directions. I usually find that at least several influences and interpretations have contributed to this new discovery about myself.

There are other times admittedly when I know of one event that has cast long shadows on me and my life. One interpretation of an event has left me a different person. In such cases there is almost a "click" of recognition. By the way, I say "interpretation" because it really isn't what happened to me, but rather what I thought happened to me that lingers on and remains active in me. As we know, it isn't what we say but what the other person hears that really counts.

Later, in a subsequent chapter, I would like to demonstrate this theory with examples from others, but first let me begin with an example about myself.

A PERSONAL EXPERIENCE WITH UNCONSCIOUS MATERIAL: THE WORKSHOP

Many years ago I made a workshop in "communications." I would guess that there were sixty or more people who came for the week-long experiential workshop. However, for interaction purposes we were divided into smaller groups of five or six. One night about the middle of the week, all sixty of us were gathered into one large room. We were seated around the walls of the rectangular room for the "music move your body exercise."

We were told that some music would be played, and only if and when we wanted to, each of us could move into the center of the room. There we were to let the music move only those physical parts of us which reacted spontaneously in response to the sounds we heard. So the music began.

About three quarters of the song was played, and I observed that no one ventured forth. The center of the room was empty. So I decided to break the ice. I went to the center of the room and began doing my most graceful pirouettes there. Rapidly the center of the room filled up with others. Some of them, I noticed, moved only their fingers. Others moved slowly and almost imperceptibly. Later we were told that the facilitators of the week were correlating "emotional openness with physical openness."

Anyway, the next morning, we were back in our small groups. Our facilitator, like a vulture, was slowly circling the small gathering. A woman in the group, whom we thought of as the "fragile lady," started to sob very audibly. Most of us, I think, had sensed that she was like a Dresden doll who would break on impact. Consequently, we spared her from all sharp-edged emotions. When she began sobbing loudly, all of us looked at the poor lady and were astonished. We wondered what had gone wrong. No one had spoken much to her. Yet, suddenly, she sat there wailing and crying huge tears. I was very moved by this, and asked her what happened. I thought I must have missed something.

Tearfully she blurted out: "Oh you know and I know that I am not participating in this group. But I just can't. It just isn't me. If I had a secret in my heart, I would gladly rip it out and show it to you." Immediately, I felt very sorry for her, and could feel myself melting with compassion. I tried to comfort her with: "C'mon. You're doing the best you can, and that's all anyone can expect of you."

Apparently our facilitator thought otherwise, and in usual (pretended at least) abrasive manner, she scolded the entire group. "You are just a bunch of patsies. 'Goo Goo Eyes' here (she had nicknames for each of us) is a master manipulator. She has been manipulating this entire group for days now and none of you has caught on."

The facilitator, whom we called the "Dragon Lady" behind her back, proceeded to explain. "There are two ways to manipulate: one, through strength, by raising one's voice. The second," she continued, "is by pretending weakness, threatening to cry or to collapse. Actually," she said, "this second way is more effective with most people. Everyone in a family usually worries about 'the baby.'"

"And this," she said, pointing to "Goo Goo Eyes," "is your baby. She has been manipulating this group for four days now. Sometimes I felt very disgusted with her. At other times I just felt sorry for her. Oh, she knows very well what to do, but she is saying she can't because she would rather cop out than cope. She has worked on this group, getting you to feel sorry for and protective of her. And this is manipulation. She prefers manipulation to honest communication."

I must admit that, at this point, my sympathies were with "Goo Goo Eyes." So I interrupted the relentless attack of "Dragon Lady" with, "Hey, don't you think you're being rather hard on her?" The facilitator snapped back at me, "Oh, shut up, Loudmouth (my nickname). You're next."

So I slunk down in my chair to get eye contact with "Goo Goo Eyes." I wanted her to know that I was on her side, and not on the side of the facilitator. When I finally made visual contact with her, "Goo Goo Eyes" surprised me. She admitted to me and to the group, "Oh, she's right. I've been doing this all my life. I say, 'I can't' because then no one will question me further. If I were to say 'I won't' someone might ask me why." Somehow I am sure it was a real moment of honesty and self-discovery in the life of "Goo Goo Eyes." She had confronted her past. At least partially, she had acknowledged her true self.

Having secured this admission from "Goo Goo Eyes," the "Dragon Lady" then moved in on me. "Well, Loudmouth," she asked rather sweetly (and therefore suspiciously), "how did it feel to be the first one up on the floor last night at the 'music-move-your-body exercise'?" I admitted that it felt rather good because others quickly followed my example. I had broken the ice successfully. The facilitator snapped back, "You know what? You've got a 'Messiah Complex.' You're determined to be a born rescuer, aren't you?"

"You did it last night for the whole group. You're doing it this morning for 'Goo Goo Eyes.' Did it ever occur to you that if you hadn't got up last night, someone else who is more shy and inhibited than you could have won a very valuable victory over self? Did it ever occur to you that 'Goo Goo Eyes' might have been able to speak up for herself? She might have said: 'Back off.

That's as much as I can take!' But no, you broke the ice
for the group, and you spoke up for 'Goo Goo Eyes.'"

I felt an immediate "click" of recognition. Her
confrontation helped me to confront myself. Something
had surfaced in me, from my unconscious world into the
conscious. I have often said that I never learned more
from someone I like less that from that facilitator. At
least, I heard myself saying "Touché" a lot. I realized that
my tendency to rescue others was as old in me as the
tendency that "Goo Goo Eyes" had to manipulate
others. In these moments of confrontation we had both
learned something about ourselves.

But the "Dragon Lady" was not through with me.
She then threw this in as an extra. "You're so dumb, I'll
bet you even give advice." I knew immediately that I had
spent much time listening to others and then giving
advice. So I asked, "What is so dumb about giving
advice?" The "Dragon Lady" responded, "You're so
dumb, you don't even know what's dumb about giving
advice." "So, please help me," I snapped with a thinly
veiled edge of impatience.

She then explained, "When one adult asks another,
'What should I do?' and the second adult tells number
one what to do, that keeps him or her weak instead of
making people strong. Instead of having to make their
own decisions, they can rely on the 'Helper.'" Then,
turning directly to me, she concluded: "You push people
out into the deep water so that you can throw them a life
preserver. 'Give a person a fish, they can eat for a day.
Teach them to fish and they can eat for a lifetime.'"
Click. Touché.

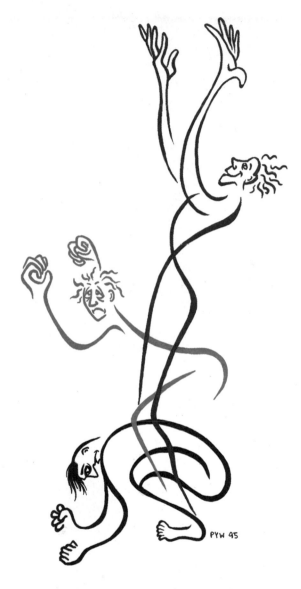

*Suffering is really a challenge
and an opportunity to grow.*

PART OF MY ACT: THE RESCUER

I have subsequently thought for a long time about my own act as a rescuer. It is embarrassingly true. I have a strong tendency to be "Mr. Fixit." I realize how I have tried to relieve others of their pain. I wanted to wave my magic wand over them, to do away with all their problems. In their moments of grief, I always tried to say to others the magical "comforting" words. And, of course, I have often felt the frustration of failure to help or to console. This for me was failure. As far as I know myself, at least in the past, I have wanted others to feel good so I could feel successful. Of course, for a long time I denied this. I repressed acknowledgment of my own needs, and rationalized that I was really helping others. I have had to revise my attitude toward suffering, to know that suffering is really a challenge and an opportunity to grow. What I had been doing in fact was preventing people from growing, so that they would be grateful to me.

Upon more mature consideration, I am now convinced that this helper role was only a part of my own adaptation. I wanted (and somehow needed) to be thought of as a "nice guy." I could console myself by thinking of all the people I had comforted and consoled, and even of those for whom I had made decisions. Instead of asking them to use their own muscles, I had kept them weak by lending out my own strength. It was a moment of insight that has helped change me. I do hope that before you finish these pages, a similar insight will occur to you. We get to know our real selves very slowly, and usually by first recognizing our roles or masks. Every insight, if accepted and acted upon, leaves us changed . . . forever.

"WHO IS DRIVING YOUR BUS?"

I have a friend, Earnie Larsen, who brings out the importance of past influences and interpretations in a very graphic way. Our yesterdays do indeed lie heavily upon our todays. Earnie asks his audiences, "Who's driving your bus?" He tells the story of a small boy who watches as his father repeatedly slaps his mother. Of course, the little boy feels totally powerless to stop his father. He can only cower under a table. He is thoroughly frightened by the spectacle of such brutality. However, inside himself, the small boy is secretly vowing, "No one will ever bully or abuse me that way!" Over the years he develops a very real antagonism for anyone trying to dominate or bully him.

Later in life, the little boy is now grown up. He is driving a bus. Suddenly he sees an approaching car veer into his lane trying to pass another car. He grits his teeth, and the old vow "No one will ever bully me that way!" explodes inside him. There is a head-on collision in which both drivers are killed.

The question is: "Who was driving that bus?" Obviously, it was the little boy. He had carried his childhood determination all the way to his grave. Now you and I must reflectively ask ourselves: "Who is driving my bus? Who is determining my actions and reactions." The truthful answer may well lie buried in our unconscious minds or world, or in our forgotten past. It might just be that a little boy or a little girl is even now pulling my strings, making many of my decisions, driving my bus. And I am not even conscious of it.

Our yesterdays do indeed lie heavily upon our todays.

QUESTIONS FOR REFLECTION

1. Our human brains really do record all our experiences. At least they record our interpretations of those experiences. If all this is true, then why is it difficult, if not foolish, to judge the responsibility of another? Can you ever judge even yourself accurately? (Distinguish actions, motivation, responsibility.)

2. Sometimes an event of our past lives is quite different from the interpretation we attached to that event. Why is it that only our "interpretation" is recorded and lingers on in us?

3. Do you tend to exercise the "power" in relationships or do you instinctively turn it over to the other person? Are you usually the "take charge" type or a "follow the leader" type?

4. Is there an event in your life similar to the "communication workshop" experience in mine? If so, what did you learn from it?

5. What is manipulation? Is there anything wrong with manipulation? Is your tendency to manipulate by strength or by weakness?

6. Is it more difficult for you to give help or to receive help? Why?

7. Why is it unwise for one adult to give advice to another adult? What is usually behind the temptation to give advice?

8. Would you rather be a "rescuer" or the "rescued"? In so-called trust-walks, would you rather be the "leader" or the "trusting

one" wearing the blindfold? What does this imply about you?

9. Who is driving the bus in your life? How does an event or series of events in your personal past influence your present behavior and decisions?

10. List the five most important and influential events of your early life. How does each affect you now?

III

Confirmation by
Examples:
Mirrors of the Past

Almost everyone I know (myself included) has mannerisms, tendencies, weaknesses and strengths. And the more I get to know people, the more I think that these mannerisms, tendencies, weaknesses and strengths are traceable to our past lives. Most times, of course, I am not sure about the sources. The only thing I am sure about is the obvious mannerism, tendency, weakness or strength. Somewhere, back in the lives of all of us, I am sure that many things happened, interpretations were made, and something kept reappearing in our reactions to life.

Of course, the one person in whom this is most obvious is myself. I can often trace my own tendencies to my past. I see some of my father's mannerisms surfacing in my own life. I see some of my mother's tendencies repeated in my own actions and reactions. I can even recall some single events which have influenced me very deeply. These events of the past shape my present behavior.

G. K. Chesterton once said that we do not know what precisely was the original sin of Adam and Eve. But we can tell from looking at human history and human beings that something went wrong. I think I can tell this, too, about my students. If they appear consistently troubled, somehow I know that something has happened in their past lives. Something has gone wrong. In the examples of this chapter this may be obvious.

My theory, therefore, is that almost all our thoughts, feelings, actions and reactions come out of something in us. And everything in us comes out of something recorded in our past. This theory is confirmed in almost everyone. Perhaps you will see it confirmed in yourself.

THE "DEPRESSION KID" AND THE "SAD FACE"

I recall getting together with an old friend. I gave him a camera to take a picture of me with his children. Well, the kids were a little antsy. They just wouldn't pose for a formal picture. After agonizing for about ten minutes the poor man gave the camera, unclicked, back to me. He explained: "You see, I am a Depression kid. I couldn't take the picture because I felt I would be wasting your film." Obviously, the "Depression kid" was driving the bus.

In another instance, I once met with one of my students. He was a handsome young man with a fine facial structure, good skin texture, and so forth. But the look on his face was strictly for a funeral. So I said to him in private, "Bob, you've got a very handsome face, but the look on your face is always so unhappy." "Yeah, I know," he moaned. As we continued to talk, he told me that he had been adopted as a baby. He knew this fact from the beginning of his life. He insisted that his adoptive parents had never ever hinted at rejection, but he assumed that if he ever displeased them in any way, they would send him back to some foster home.

He went on to tell me that the only person who had loved him in a way that made him feel totally accepted was his adoptive grandmother. She died when he was six years old.

On her deathbed, little Bobby pleaded with her: "Don't die, Grandma." She replied, "Oh, Bobby, I have to die sometime. Besides, you're going to make it." "Oh, I can't, Grandma." He added that when she did die, "It was like someone had turned out all the lights in my world." Suddenly I could understand the pained look on his face. It was the look of a little boy who was asking: "Are you going to send me back to a foster home?" It was the little boy pleading with his grandmother: "Please don't die, Grandma." A little boy was now driving the bus of his life. It is a little boy who still looks at the world with a pained expression on his face.

A little boy was now driving the bus
of his life.

AN EXPLOSION AND A DISAGREEMENT IN CLASS

One day, another of my students exploded in class. We had been talking about "delusion." I had said, "We are all a little or a lot deluded, but all of us are somewhat deluded." It was at this point that the explosion occurred. The young man in question shouted out: "The church has deluded us. You have deluded us." After the initial explosion he refused to talk. Later, he told me privately that his father was a minister and the pastor of a church. He had always wanted to be close to his father, but his mother always seemed to interpose herself. He also implied that he was homosexual.

He continued: "I was the kind of kid you liked to beat up. So every day, after school, I took my beating and went home." Once I had learned the background of the young man, I could better understand the explosion in class. All that anger was gathering in him as a child trying to be close to his father, and in a boy being beaten up every day after school. It was an old anger that exploded in class that day. The little boy was still in full control, driving the bus of his life, heading for disaster.

Another time one of the young men in my class informed me that he disagreed with "everything" I had to say. I gulped at the word *everything*. Anyway, I later found out that when he was five years old, his mother awakened him and told him he had to go live with his father, from whom she was divorced. "I've got a job with a pension now, and I can't raise you any more." He later told me: "I felt rejected by my own mother when I was five years old. Early on in my teen years I got involved with drugs. I've been sour on everything and everybody ever since." Our yesterdays indeed lie heavily upon our todays. Perhaps someday this young man will be able to let go of this old anger. I can only hope that as an adult he will take the steering wheel out of the hands of the child who was rejected by his own mother when he was only five years old.

THE ABBOT . . . AND MY FRIEND

Thomas Keating was an abbot in a cloistered monastery in Spencer, Massachusetts. In his book *Open Mind, Open Heart,* he remembers his days as abbot. He said that many of the men under his leadership seemed to be dealing with their parents rather than with himself. Almost all of us have these juvenile "hangovers." We displace our logjammed emotion on the wrong people and the wrong issues. Everything that has ever happened to us is somewhere recorded on our brains. Whenever we act or react, these messages and memories impel us into certain actions or reactions. If we are to change, everything must start here, with this acknowledgment: Whatever is recorded in us in the past affects our later lives.

In my own younger days I had a friend who has since lost his mind. We have kept in touch over the years. In his lucid moments he is very honest and forthright about his mental illness. Once while we were visiting, during one of these clearer times, I asked him if his doctors did any psychotherapy on him. "Have they searched for something inside you that has caused your pain?" His answer was: "No, once they classify you as insane, they give up on your ability to give them helpful answers. So they just drug and medicate us. They ask questions like: 'Are you sleeping well?' and so forth?" So I candidly asked him if he ever put such searching, therapeutic questions to himself.

"Oh," he replied, "all I can remember is that I stayed at school as long as I could. I didn't want to go home." So I asked, "And what was at home that was hard to live with?" "My mother!" he nearly shouted. "She constantly corrected me. Whenever company came over to our house, as soon as they departed, she would list all my social errors." Then, because his particular psychosis is religious exaggeration, he became very scrupulous. "Oh, I shouldn't have said that . . . not about my own mother." I tried in vain to assure him that he was only telling me about the impressions he got. They may not have been facts. But the adolescent boy in him had a firm grip on the steering wheel. Memories, impressions from the past were and are in charge of his present life and of his mind.

THE LADY WHO WAS LIKED OR DISLIKED . . . AND THE TWO BROTHERS

On another occasion I was talking with an older woman. She began every sentence about another person with, "I think he likes me. . . . I think she doesn't like me. . . ." I gently called her attention to this, and she immediately said, "Oh, that's my mother. She always said, 'If you dress (or talk or think) like that, people will (or won't) like you.'" This woman herself is getting along in years, but the mother of her childhood is still waving a finger in her face, lecturing her about whether or not people will or won't like her.

I once knew two brothers. The older one was always angry, and often his anger spilled out on his "kid brother." There was a difference of two or three years in their ages. I was telling a psychiatrist friend of mine about them, and he shocked me. "The younger brother stole mommy away from the older one." "He did?" I gasped. "How do you know that?" My psychiatrist friend asked me to picture a two-year-old standing looking at the lap he once sat in. A new baby is being held there now. The older one feels rejected. He wonders, "Where did this new kid come from? Why is he getting all the 'kootchy koos' I used to get?"

I interjected that the older boy seemed to be the favorite child of both parents. I got a psychiatric smile of recognition, "Oh, that's a lot of responsibility to place on the shoulders of a little kid, isn't it? You know, 'You're the favorite. You're the one we're counting on.'" I had never thought of this before, but it is still another example of a child driving the bus through an adult life. So I asked my psychiatrist friend, "The men are in their late fifties now. Could that childhood resentment still be in the older boy? And could he still feel the responsibility of being the favorite?" I shall never forget the answer: "Oh yes, unless he has talked it out and confronted his own behavior."

THE PRISONER OF SECOND AVENUE

I am told that art imitates life. Earlier I mentioned that this book is the product of my own life and efforts. I even admitted that I once thought that this book would be superfluous. But I didn't tell you about the experience that actually started me writing. Strangely, it was an old movie, *The Prisoner of Second Avenue*. It was an art-form portrayal of two brothers. One of them (Jack Lemmon) loses his mind. He then goes to a psychiatrist, who is unfortunately portrayed as a sad and detached man. However, in the course of therapy with this man, Jack Lemmon somehow discovers the pattern of his own behavior that still clings to him. "I made a surrogate father of others and always tried to please them. I never fought back." He saw himself as a "people pleaser."

Later in the movie, when he and his older brother are arguing, they instinctively go back to their childhood. They argue about a picture taken at the time, and about who got the privileged position in the picture. They argue about who was the favorite child in the family. Quite naturally, they both identify the other as the favorite child in the family. Jack Lemmon insists that he had put the older brother in place of their deceased father. Of course, in the movie Jack Lemmon confronts his past and he does find his way back into sanity. However, it was the "argument" scene that convinced me to write. Small boys were still driving the buses of those two adult lives. Old aggravations were still seething inside of both. We do have long memories, don't we? Our yesterdays do in fact lie heavily upon our todays.

THE TYRANT AND WARDEN . . . AND THE "TOUGH GUY"

Still another friend of mine, after he was married, became a "tyrant and warden." This was his wife's description of him. My friend insisted that his wife and children had to obey his rules. You know, "Little Caesar has spoken. Let no dog bark back." I happened to know that

*The power struggle between his parents has
cast a meaningful shadow over his
own life and present behavior.*

this man came from a family in which his mother had all the power. She completely dominated her husband. By strength or by weakness she dominated not only her husband but the whole flock. This usually results in unresolved anger on the part of the flock. However, since the man in question never really has confronted this part of his past, there is no "for sureness" about this situation. But in my own observation, the unresolved anger resulting in his consequent domination is a strong possibility. The power struggle between his parents has cast a meaningful shadow over his own life and present behavior.

I suspect that this man unconsciously knew of his mother's domination, and was determined that "this will never happen to me." Like the little boy cowering under the table, he is determined that "no one will ever bully me like that." If I am right, the resolution of a small boy still prompts most of the urges, makes most of the decisions for an adult man.

Another example. I remember once being approached by a man who appeared to be very "tough." (He buttoned his shirt only at the navel. He talked out of the corner of his mouth.) He mentioned to me that he had been in "Nam" (Vietnam), where he had a nervous breakdown. He told me that he was put into a veterans' hospital, and injected with truth serum. The interview that followed was recorded on a film, which he later saw. The person he saw in the film was very gentle and loving. "Who the hell is that?" he asked. The doctors replied, "That is the real you. You had to put a mask over your tenderness to do and to live with what you had to do in Vietnam. You are still wearing that mask." Your yesterdays are controlling your todays, they might have said.

I have not seen him since, but I do hope he has allowed his true self to emerge. Otherwise, he will just shadowbox and spin his wheels for the rest of his life. The same thing is true of you and me. Yesterday (Yesteryears) and its experiences usually explain our reactions to today. At least this will be true until we ask ourselves the right questions and confront our own reality. Someone from the past may be piloting our course through life.

QUESTION FOR REFLECTION

Did you find something to which you resonated in the examples of:

The Depression Kid

The Boy with the Sad Face

The Kid Who Wanted to Be Close to His Minister Father

The Boy Who Was Rejected at Age Five by His Mother

The Abbot and His Monks

My Friend Who Lost His Mind

The Lady Who Was Liked or Disliked

The Older Brother and His Kid Brother

The Two Brothers in *The Prisoner of Second Avenue*

The Tyrant and Warden

The Tough Guy from "Nam"

IV

The Solution:
Ownership!

We are complicated. Our yesterdays lie heavily upon our todays. So what can we do about it? Before we get into the solution, there are two prior questions that everyone must consider. The first of these is this: Can people really change? When we turn the well-worn pages of the album of our lives, we probably find very few people who have changed. Most people just become "more so," more of what they always were. For this reason we must ask ourselves: Can people change? In our life experience we probably can think of some who really did change. And, from the fact that some people have really changed, the possibility of change cannot be denied. Anyway, the second prior

question is this: Do I really want to change? Oh,
change can occur if I work at it. But do I really
want to know myself and change what I can? Do
I have the courage and determination to free
myself? These are the questions most of us must
ponder as we begin to work toward greater self-
knowledge.

AN "OWNER," NOT A "BLAMER" — AND A CAUTION

The starting point for all true self-knowledge is ownership. I must acquire new habits of thinking and speaking.
I must acknowledge that all my actions, reactions and
feelings come out of something in me. I may not always
have faucet-control over these things. And I certainly do
not mean to imply any moral responsibility. Still, I have
to own whatever is in me. It is a part of me, however it
got there. I must never place the blame at another's feet.
I must never shift this solemn and personal responsibility
onto someone else or something else. My behavior and
my feelings are mine! They are always the product of
something in me. If I truly accept this, I will instinctively
make "I" rather than "You" statements. I will never say,
"You hurt me." Only this, "I felt hurt."

A much-needed word of caution here. I must
eliminate the word *blame* from my thoughts and vocabulary. It is most important that I do not blame others for
my reactions and equally important that I do not blame
myself. I must presume myself innocent until proven
guilty, and a guilty verdict calls for a judgment which I
simply cannot make. In taking responsibility for my

I have to own whatever is in me.

behaviors and feelings, I simply acknowledge that they come from something in me. It could understandably help me if I knew how this "something" got into me, but I may never know its exact source or origin.

Let us suppose that I am a bit oversensitive to criticism, a bit defensive. How did I get that way? Did someone model this for me and I simply imitated them? And did I consequently accept it into my own collection of attitudes? Was I told that I must be above all criticism? Did I make the interpretation somewhere along the way that all criticism is ultimately destructive criticism? Do I secretly think that people who criticize me just don't like me? However it happened, I must open my arms to the child of my past and not carry a judgmental knife with which to gouge out my heart. It may well be that I innocently got the wrong idea somewhere, sometime. In claiming ownership of my behaviors and feelings, I must proceed with curiosity and love the self I am trying to know. I must proceed with open, sympathetic arms, eliminating the concept of "blame" from my very thoughts and consequently the word from my vocabulary.

OWNERSHIP OF BEHAVIOR

We have said that we must exercise ownership over both behaviors and feelings. First, let's take the easier one: behaviors. You may well have already heard my favorite story to illustrate this. (Well, I guess you're going to hear it again!) It concerns the late Sidney Harris, a syndicated columnist. It seems that Harris and a friend were going to a newsstand so that Harris's friend could buy a newspaper. The man selling the papers was his usual self: mean and angry. However, the friend of Harris was unflappably nice to him. In his parting remark he wished the paper vendor "a happy day." To which the poor, disgruntled man replied, "Don't tell me what kind of day to have. I have other plans."

So Harris inquired, "Is that guy always so mean?"

"Yes, unfortunately he is."

"And are you always so nice to him?"

"Yes, of course."

"Why, if he is always so mean, are you always so nice?"

Harris's friend had to think for a while. The answer seemed obvious to him. Finally, he said, "Because I don't want him to decide how I am going to act. I must decide that. You see, I am an actor, not a reactor." Harris admitted in a subsequent column that at first he was a bit astonished. Then he thought, "This is one of the big lessons to be learned in life. Be an actor, not a reactor."

The difference between these two options is obvious. Actors decide how they are going to act. Reactors let other people, other situations, the group, or perhaps the barometer, decide for them.

We ask honestly, "Aren't there situations in which everyone would react the same way?" The answer is simply NO! When we say (as most of us have), "Well, anyone would have . . ." we are simply wrong. This is very important. I must decide for myself how I am going to act. I am a free human being, not an automatic, other-controlled robot.

"You can always tell a teacher," so the saying goes, "but you can't tell them much." Anyway, as a teacher's device I have asked this question of my classes: "If I don't like you, but I am very nice to you, am I being honest?

Actors decide how they are going to act.

Am I being myself?" My answer is, of course, YES! I know, as a teacher, that the one or two in my class who need love the most are probably the least attractive. They act as though they need love the least. The shy person doesn't want to be involved. The angry person challenges almost everything. These are the people who most need my love and kindness. The hurt person needs my understanding, not another put-down. So I must decide how I am going to act. And often I have to act against my feelings. In loving those I do not like I am being my truest self, because I have decided to make my life an act of love. I am convinced that only love really helps people.

Earlier we mentioned the Transactional Analysis theory of Erich Berne. According to this theory, the secret of a successful life is to keep one's adult in charge of one's life. You will remember: P–A–C, Parent–Adult–Child. We must never let the messages on our parent tapes or the emotions of the child in us make decisions for us. I must always keep the adult in me in charge—my mind thinking independently and my will choosing a course of behavior for itself. I must decide how I am going to act. And I must take full responsibility for all my actions.

OWNERSHIP OF FEELINGS

Now let's get to the harder question: the feelings. Sometimes feelings arise so quickly and spontaneously that we think of them as automatic and natural. I once thought that feelings were like sneezes. They come and go harmlessly. They are really not very important. Now I think that feelings are critically important in good communication and they are diagnostic of what is really in us. I now know that my feelings point to what is really in me. They help me "diagnose" my deepest attitudes and values as nothing else can.

The important thing, here and now, is that all my feelings come from something in me. And they tell me something about myself. Even my so-called mood swings are diagnostic. No one else and nothing else can produce a specific feeling in me. No person or thing can make me angry unless there is already anger in me. Likewise, other persons or things cannot make me joyful unless there is already some joy in me. Others can only stimulate what is already in me.

Eleanor Roosevelt, the wife of President Franklin D. Roosevelt, had a sign on the wall of her office which read: NO ONE CAN MAKE YOU FEEL INFERIOR WITHOUT YOUR PERMISSION. I have to feel inferior to others before someone can stimulate these feelings in me. If I don't feel inferior to others, but someone says or implies this, I can only scratch my head and wonder, How could the person have come to such a mistaken conclusion?

Another teacher's device: I ask my students, "If someone were to walk out of class on me, stamping his or her foot, demanding tuition back, how do you think I would feel?" The first student to answer says something like: "Oh, I suppose you would feel angry. You know, like, 'You're going to pay for this, Kid. I've got your social security number.'" Then I turn to the next student, with the same question, only the answer is usually different: "I think you would feel hurt, like, 'How could he do this to me? I was doing the best I could.'" A third student may react by telling me that I would feel compassionate: "Poor kid isn't ready for this, eh?"

When I have listened to about a dozen different answers, I usually add, "You know, I would probably react in one of the ways just mentioned. Only I'm not sure which. But there is one thing I would know: It wasn't the student walking out who caused my feelings. Something in me—some hidden fear, anger or virtue—was stimu-lated and so I reacted in one of those ways. Some people might have reactions like mine, but others would react quite differently, I'm sure. Because of my individuality and the unique things in me, my reactions will always be like my fingerprints: only mine.

SUMMARY

So the beginning of a solution is ownership of my behaviors and feelings. I must let my behaviors and feelings tell me about who I really am. In order to be a good listener to my behaviors and feelings, I must remember to eliminate the word *blame* from my thinking and from my vocabulary. As has already been said, if I am ready to judge myself harshly or to blame myself, I will very likely be dishonest. I will be tempted to revert to shifting the responsibility to someone else, to blame.

In order to find my true self, I must have the desire to know the truth. But if I find that the truth will be more that I think I can bear, I will try to avoid confronting it. So I have to approach this matter calmly and curiously rather that judgmentally. I must not have blood in my eyes or flames snorting out of my nostrils.

*If I find that the truth will be more
than I think I can bear, I will try
to avoid confronting it.*

THE GHOSTS OF MY PAST: INTERPRETATIONS THAT HAVE LINGERED

The second part of my own theory, as you may recall, is that everything that comes out of me comes out of something in my past. There are two steps to this process. Something may have happened to me or have been modeled for me in the past. But to get inside me, it had to pass through the filter of my own interpretation. As is often repeated in courses on communication: "It isn't what you say but what others hear that affects them."

I remember presiding at a liturgy for a family. One of the little boys present had not yet made his First Communion. So when I was distributing the hosts, I passed him by. At the end of the Mass, I saw his lower lip protruding a bit and asked him if anything was wrong. Finally, after denying that anything was wrong, he burst into tears. He blurted out: "You passed me by because you don't like me." "Oh, Matthew," I added quickly, "nothing could be further from the truth. You are one of the finest young men I know." I then explained how he would someday join his classmates in receiving his First Holy Communion. But I have often thought that if I had not noticed the lower lip quivering, the misinterpretation might have become permanent. We might have passed like two ships in the night. A single event could have cast a long shadow over Matthew's young life.

In another instance, I know of a woman who admits to feeling estranged from her mother throughout adolescence. She felt this distance because "My mother didn't cry when my father died." Later, the daughter discovered that her mother had actually shed many tears in private. But she had tried to keep a "stiff upper lip" in front of her children. The daughter discovered a series of letters that her mother had written to her deceased husband. These letters spoke of the deep feelings and much grieving. This, of course, reversed the daughter's earlier judgments and misinterpretations. The fact is: We do interpret—rightly or wrongly—whatever we experience. And it is this interpretation that tends to persevere or linger in us. This is why we must learn to reevaluate our past experiences, and to revise our previous interpretations.

Another example of misinterpretation that comes to mind is my own tendency to animate the inanimate and then to scold it. Lightbulbs that don't screw in easily and objects that roll off my desk onto the floor are among my favorites. But there are many others: things I can't quite reach, paper that jams in the copier, things I stub my toes on, and books or papers that I just can't find, to name only a few. When these things upset the smoothness of life, I scold them for frustrating me.

I recall that my father had this same habit, and we children used to try to hide our laughter. How silly, we thought. When in my own adult years I find myself repeating this habit, I guess I know from whom it came. In fact, I am certain. I am my father's son. Of course, I now understand my father and his "silly" habit in a new way. Everything that appears in us has a history. This is true of my father, of me, and of you. I like to think that everyone makes psychological if not logical sense.

AN IMPORTANT PART OF THE THEORY: THE INNER OBSERVER

The theory that I have been advancing goes this way. I must own everything I do, say and feel. Of course, I may be totally innocent but I have to admit that something in me requires an "inner observer" who is honest but at the same time sympathetic. That is essential to the theory.

An important thing about this "something in me" is that it goes back, maybe way back, in my life. As was said, it may have been modeled for me by someone I chose to imitate, or it may have resulted from the way I was treated at an early stage of my life. But it had to be something on which I passed some kind of judgment, or something of which I made some kind of interpretation or misinterpretation.

So how do I gain greater self-knowledge in order to change and grow? I would like to suggest that the process goes like this. I must let each day of life question me, and my "inner observer" must notice my own responses. As I encounter various people, as events occur in my life, and as my feelings emerge I keep observing myself in action. My "inner observer" must be honest in what it sees and sympathetic (not harshly judgmental) in understanding my feelings, actions and reactions.

Whatever I observe in myself I need to own. I must claim as products of something in me all my behaviors and all my feelings. Then I need to move from today's events into the past to see what original events may become mirrors of reflection for me. Is my response today a reflection of yesterday? Why? What happened then? How did I interpret it? What effect does it have today? Can I change that? Do I really want to?

As you read the following examples, apply this process and see what personal profit results for you.

*I must let each day of life question me,
and my "inner observer" must
notice my own responses.*

DON'T MAKE WAVES

Two young women in my class had the look of zombies. They said very little, never showed any emotion, just seemed to be taking up time and space. Later, and separately, I found out that both were "adult children of alcoholics." In each case the father had been the drinker, and during the adolescence of the young women their fathers had stopped drinking. But, as one of the young women explained, "The messages remain on my parent-tapes. 'Don't talk, feel, or make any waves. Pretend that you're a picture on the wall or something. Otherwise, Daddy may throw a tantrum.'"

The "inner observer" in each woman had to make her person aware that these present habits go way back to childhood. Messages had been given and personally interpreted. Habits were begun. A frightened child was driving the bus. Now, as adults, these two women must acknowledge and own their behaviors and feelings. Then with sympathetic understanding they will need to begin to change, to act on their insights, in order to grow out of the legacy of their pasts.

NEVER, NEVER MAKE A MISTAKE

A friend of mine who went through the seminary with me candidly admits, "I can sing, dance, and perform in public. But I can't read." You see, in the seminary we had reading at lunch and dinner, so while the rest of us were eating, one of our number would read to us. About his fear of reading in public, my friend explained, "I keep waiting for the old prefect of reading to catch me in a mistake and shout out 'Repetat!' ('Let it be repeated!')."

He had traced back his own inability to read in public to the prefect of reading suddenly interrupting to point out a mistake or mispronunciation. The question of change is this: Who will continue to drive my friend's bus?

THE FEAR OF GOD

I once knew two sisters who in their adult years wanted nothing to do with religion. As soon as the subject was brought up, they changed the topic of conversation. I was very much aware of this and figured that something must have happened in their childhood to have cast such a regrettable shadow over religion and their relationship with God. Finally, the younger of the two sisters married and moved out of state. For some reason she started writing to me. She admitted that she was taking up religious practice again, but always had nightmares before going to church. For the first time, she told me about her mother, who had long since been dead. She vividly described moments of insanity in her mother. She told me that her mother would approach her with a cross, and press it into her little child's flesh, "to drive the devil out of you." As an adult, she asked in writing: "Do you think I am possessed by the devil?" Suddenly, everything fell into place. The aversion for religion went all the way back to her very early years. Today, she is an actor, not a reactor—an owner, not a blamer. She is working to reinterpret her image of God and that relationship.

THE DRUMMER BOY

On another occasion, one of my young students claimed he was hyperactive. He always sat right under me, in the first row. He fidgeted, played drummer boy, talked to the girl sitting next to him. Finally, other students came to me with objections to his presence and noise in class. So he and I finished the course tutorially. I met with him on an individual basis. In the course of our meetings, we became good friends. He admitted to me that he had been on drugs, and was currently in therapy. He told his therapist about me and taking the theology course tutorially. Eventually, he and his therapist came to the conclusion that he "did not want to hear" what I was saying in class. So unbeknownst to himself, and certainly to me, he made noises to distract himself, the class and me. He did this unconsciously, until he traced his present behavior back to an earlier point in his own life. He owned his own behavior and feelings, and allowed them to question him about his past.

AN ACCIDENT THAT KEEPS REPEATING ITSELF

I know an elderly lady who has a quavering voice. She sounds as though she expects something bad to happen. I always wondered about her childhood. On one occasion, she told me that her father was alcoholic. In an intoxicated condition, he had been hit by a car when returning home one evening. After he recuperated from his injuries, the daughter was preoccupied with the possibility of a recurrence of such an accident. She admitted that she was always "relieved" when Daddy made it home uninjured. Something in me is sure that her present uncertain voice and manner go back to this anxious childhood experience. Today, the full enjoyment of life is blocked by the emotions of yesterday.

HOW LONG IS "FOREVER"?

Another time, I was scheduled to hear the wedding vows of a young couple whom I had taught. A month or so before the scheduled wedding, the couple came to me. She was in tears. She was on the verge of backing out of the wedding. It sounded like more than the usual "nuptial jitters." She continually asked him if their marriage bond was "forever," and if he would be a faithful husband. They eventually left, but I'm sure she still had her quivering emotions. They were married, and at the wedding reception I found out that earlier on her father had left her mother and married a much younger woman. I'm sure that the divorce in her own family of origin had much to do with her doubts just before her own wedding. She must learn to see her emotions as the residue of past experiences. She must learn to separate her marriage from her parents' marriage. Only then can an adult drive the bus of her life.

AN ADULT CHILD OF PARANOIA

My last example of something that "goes back" in one's life is that of a young student. She clearly was high on the paranoia scale. She consistently interpreted almost everything as a personal attack on herself. Everyone was out "to get her." One day as she was telling me about the latest of these persecution attacks, I asked her if anyone in her family was paranoid. She smiled knowingly, and told me about her father. Poor man. Everything that was done in his own life was done to "trick him." I asked her if maybe she had modeled herself on her father in this regard. Again, the knowing smile. The click that her own paranoia went back to her earlier childhood. In this moment of recognition is the promise of freedom. She can learn to laugh at her "persecution feelings" or let them continue to control her.

My point in telling you all these stories is this. You and I must own our present behaviors and feelings and see them as coming from something in us. Then, if we trace that "something" back into our own past, we will get to know ourselves. From here on, change and growth are possible. "Name it, claim it, and then share it" has become my formula for getting to know myself.

TWO FINAL WORDS ON THE SUBJECT

The first final word is to reiterate the caution about not blaming, others or myself. I can't blame others because I do not know if they actually did or said to me what my own interpreting memory tells me. It is also true that I can't get at their historical motives. Maybe they were trying to do their best. Nor should I blame myself. Maybe it was actually as I remember it, maybe not. Why I imitated a given mannerism or interpreted something as I did is really not a fair question. I just can't know. The only fair question concerns my willingness to accept responsibility for my own behavior and emotions. I must not let the child in me remain at the steering wheel of my life. I must now take over the driving of my own bus. I must put my own adult in charge of my life. Under God, I must be the master of my own fate. I am the person responsible for my own happiness. Whenever I look into a mirror, I am looking at the face of a person who is responsible for whether or not I have a good day, and life.

The second (and last) word is this. If I do become an owner and not a blamer, an actor and not a reactor, I will gradually get to know myself. This means that I will have to give up pretense as far as possible. I will have to act on my own honest insights. I will have to be myself. I will have to communicate honestly and openly. (Actually, when you think about it, the only real gift I have to give is myself. Everything else is just token.)

Only in this way can I get to know more about my true self. Owners do. Blamers do not. Actors do. Reactors don't. Honesty does. Pretense does not.

So what do we do? I mean, where do I start? Read on. The last chapter will help reduce this plateful to practice.

QUESTIONS FOR REFLECTION

1. Who in my life has really changed? Who has just become "more so"?
2. Why is self-observation without blaming so helpful to self-understanding?
3. In what situations do I let other people or situations control my decisions?
4. Have I ever acknowledged that my feelings or emotions come out of something in me? In what situations do I tend to blame others for my emotions?
5 Do I agree with Eleanor Roosevelt's sign: "NO ONE CAN MAKE YOU FEEL INFERIOR WITHOUT YOUR PERMIS- SION"? In what circumstances do I allow myself to feel inferior?

6. What is meant by an "Inner Observer" and why is it so essential?

7. What can I point to in my past that results in my present pattern of behavior and/or feelings?

8. Why are we really responsible for our own happiness? Is happiness something we can choose? Why or why not?

9. If I am a "blamer" and "reactor," why will I never know myself?

10. Why do "owners" and "actors" get to know themselves?

V

The Practice: Self-Knowledge Through Action

Some people are inclined to speculation. They ask things like, "How many angels can dance on the head of a pin?" Most of us, however, are not so inclined. We want to know how this—whatever it is—fits into life, my life. We think of ourselves as practical people. We ask only, "How much will this cost me?"

There is, of course, another side of us. It just doesn't want to pay the price, to make the effort. If there were a magic wand, which could produce self-knowledge immediately, we would want it waved over us and our lives. But the old saying has it that "It works if you work at it." Most of us

tend to begrudge the effort it takes to restructure
our lives to develop new habits. We just don't
like the work it takes. We just don't seem to have
the patience.

At the same time, we are fascinated with
ourselves. We have asked so many questions
about ourselves. We have engaged in many
interior debates that others couldn't hear or even
suspect. We have many unanswered questions.
This effort at self-knowledge can be very interesting.

Dag Hammarskjöld has said that the longest
journey is the journey inward. But we do meet
many familiar signposts along the road. A lot of
it is familiar knowledge. A lot of it is fun. It's
something like solving a mystery. And most of us
are nothing if not mysterious. I guess the advice
is true: "Begin. Everything else is easy." Once we
begin, momentum seems to take over, to carry us
along.

First of all, I want to say that not all practice has been
confined to this chapter. If you have consistently been
answering or discussing the various questions at the end
of each chapter, you have already been putting the
theory into practice.

As was suggested, the place to begin is within
ourselves. We should work at self-responsibility and
develop an "inner observer." We must strive to become
actors, not reactors; owners, not blamers.

Psychiatrist Viktor Frankl makes a good point, I
think, when he suggests that I let life question me.

*The longest journey
is the journey inward.*

Instead of waking up each morning, and wondering about what the day will bring to me, I must wake up wondering about what questions life will ask me today. For example, do I really believe that obnoxious behavior is a cry of pain, an appeal for help? Life may ask that question of me when an obnoxious person enters my daily give and take. Do I really believe that people are more important than things? Life may well ask me that question today when some person wants to borrow one of my cherished things. Or life may ask me if I can love those I see as unlovable. Sometimes I feel sure that we know that the person who most needs our love is the person least likely to ask for it, or to win it. Indeed, we must be willing to be asked questions by life. If I do practice self-responsibility, and I do let life question me, I am bound to find out some previously unknown things about myself. Only then can I do something about this newfound self-knowledge.

PRACTICE ONE: TALKING IT OVER

If I develop an "inner observer" and allow life to question me, I surely will come up with some success at self-discovery. For example, my inner observer may ask me, "Why did I react in the way I did?" Or, "Was it that other person's problem or mine?" "What were the deeper reasons for my feelings in the matter?" "Do men and women really speak a different language?" Men seem to achieve their identity through facts, women through relationships. Men tend to put down women for "thinking," but women are more intuitive than men. How does all this apply to me and my relationships?

Even if we try to be honest and reflective, we may still be missing the main message of our inner observer. We are so easily deceived. At some point, it is very necessary to talk over my opinions or judgments with another person. Inside myself, I can so easily suppress the truth, rationalize or deny the obvious. But with another, if I really want to confide in that person, denial is less likely. Another person can see through my defenses as I cannot. Another can be more objective about me than I can be.

Of course, it is important that the other person be balanced, nonjudgmental and very honest. It is much easier to lie to myself than to another. When I have to put all the pieces on the desk or table between us, it is more difficult to rearrange those pieces or keep some of them concealed. I can do this when I keep things inside myself. As the poet John Berryman said, "We are as sick as we are secret." I can know myself only if I have the courage to confide my hiddenness to another.

The first thing that occurs to most of us is that there is no such confidant or would-be confidant in our lives. Maybe this, too, is a rationalized answer. We may want it to be true because it closes the door to self-honesty and self-confrontation, at least to talking things over with a friend.

There is such a thing, however, as "reevaluation," or "co-counseling." Let me pass it on in the way it was explained to me. First, I must seek out a partner for this. It should be someone I trust, someone I can share with most comfortably. Once we agree upon the partnership and the amount of time each exchange will take (fifteen or twenty minutes), we can proceed.

We are as sick as we are secret.

What we do is share some incident or perhaps a relationship issue from our past lives during which we felt constrained not to express our feelings. Ah! but now in hindsight we can go back and look into the past with more objective eyes. We can at last express all the feelings that we could not express at the time of the incident or during the relationship.

For example, "I wet my pants in second grade. I felt so terribly embarrassed and angry at the teacher who told me to wait until recess. But I could not express either my embarrassment or anger at the time. But now I can." And so I do. The other person does not actively "counsel" me. The only questions to be asked are those that will clarify my sharing. "How long have you felt that way? Was this the most significant embarrassment of your childhood? How does this affect you in your life today?" And so forth.

After the agreed amount of time for the first person has been used, the other person is invited to do the same type of sharing. For example, "I thought the question my boyfriend was going to ask me pertained to marriage, and I was all ready to say 'yes.' Instead, he asked if our relationship really had a future. I was surprised, hurt, angry, and even felt a bit guilty all at the same time." This second person continues to share in the same way the first did. And for the same amount of time.

Does this kind of sharing help? Yes, without a doubt, it does. Releasing even the older emotions of yesteryear helps break the logjam. Also, it makes us more free to express our emotions of the moment, instead of repressing, rationalizing or denying them. But breaking the logjam of emotions also does something else. It helps to clear up my vision, to objectify my attitudes. It brings me to a deeper understanding of myself. And this will stimulate new growth in me.

There is, of course, no substitute for the honest desire to know oneself. Any good psychotherapist knows that what is really important is that the client, not the therapist, see the truth. I suspect that most good therapists know the truth about their clients before the clients do themselves. But it does no good until the patient recognizes the truth and acts on it. In reevaluation, or co-counseling, what is important is that the speaker see the truth by sharing it. It is of less importance that the listener grasp the truth of the speaker. I think that, if one truly wants to see the truth, to know oneself better, this will be the inevitable result.

However, this moment of realized truth may take some time. As every good therapist knows, the "presenting" problem is probably not the "real" problem. In other words, the problem that the person comes in with is probably not the real problem that the person will eventually identify.

Certainly, it is important to put out all the pieces. I must see how they fit together. When I do, there will gradually appear the dawn of self-discovery. Another person may supply the needed connectives, but only by empathic presence or by asking sympathetic questions. For example, "Did you ever think that maybe your father or mother modeled this quality for you?" "What happened at the time in your life when you changed so much?" Questions like these demonstrate the importance of finding someone for a sharing-partner who is honest but not judgmental. The questions of a good, empathic listener may stimulate new insights in the speaker.

In the relatively rare situation in which there is no such person, then one must seek out a warm and receptive group, like Al-Anon or Growth or Emotions Anonymous. However, the group must abide by the honest, nonjudgmental standards proposed for individual confidants. There are such groups in almost all communities.

PRACTICE TWO: TURNING IT OVER — "IN GOD WE TRUST"

In some groups that I have heard about over the years, there is what they call the "God-box." This is the way it was explained to me. The important, implied suggestion about this box is that you don't try to shoulder all your own concerns, decisions and worries. These are entrusted to the Higher Power of God. Each person writes out a "problem" and then ceremoniously puts it into the God-box. From that point on, it is in the hands of God.

This practice might well seem to be a "cop-out." However, I would like to quote the Jewish author, Franz Werfel, who wrote in his foreword to *The Song of Bernadette*: "For those who believe, no explanation is necessary. For those who do not believe, no explanation is possible." Before a successful "turning it all over to God" is possible, one must believe that God really does want us to be happy. Also, we must believe that God controls the circumstances of our lives, really does pull the strings of our life-events. As Lacordaire once said,

"All I know of tomorrow is this, that Providence will rise before the sun."

However, we must also ask God to educate our instincts. We have to do our part. "Pray as though every-thing depends on God. But work as though everything depends on you." Another version of the same truth says: "If you are out at sea in a small boat and a storm arises, pray as though everything depends on God, but keep rowing for the shore." In other words, in turning it over to God, we must ask God to inspire us to use our own skills, to make a personal effort. We must ask God to illu-minate and empower us to cooperate in our efforts at self-knowledge and growth. But the final solution is God's. The outcome is always left in God's hands.

"Worry," it has been said, "is like being in a rocking chair. It doesn't get you anywhere, but it gives you something to do." It is this needless worry or concern that is forsaken in turning the whole matter over to God. In the groups mentioned earlier, if one returns to worrying, the person in search of self-knowledge must remove the paper on which he or she has written out the concern, and must carry it around. It is redeposited in the God-box only when that person is ready to give God all the pieces, ready to leave the outcome completely in God's hands.

To illustrate this point, let me summarize here the story of Bill Wilson, cofounder of Alcoholics Anonymous. Bill was a hopeless alcoholic. He had been dried out innumerable times by his physician, a Doctor William Silkworth. Finally, Doctor Silkworth confronted him with a final diagnosis: "Bill, you are a hopeless alcoholic.

All I know of tomorrow is this,
that Providence will rise
before the sun.

There is nothing more that I can do for you. I can't go on just taking your money." So Bill asked his doctor, "Is there anything I can do?" Doctor Silkworth said, "Look, I am a man of science, not of the cloth. But the famous psychiatrist Carl Jung says that a religious experience is the only hope for drinkers like you." It seems that Doctor Jung had another patient who had some kind of experience of God's power. He was sober from the very moment of his experience.

So Bill Wilson returned to his room in the hospital and said aloud, "God, I don't know if I even believe in you. But if you are there, please help me. You are my only hope." That was the moment of his spiritual experience. In the movie *My Name Is Bill W.*, he tells his cofounder, Doctor Bob Smith, "The experience has passed but the peace remains." Anyway, Bill knew at the moment of his own religious experience that he would never take another drink. And, of course, he never did. There are many stories to tell about people turning their lives, or at least a given problem, over to God. I tend to be a little skeptical of some of these stories, but there are those like that of Bill Wilson in which the intervention of God seems undeniable.

One question that recurs to me is this: Why do some people experience the presence, power and intervention of God, and others do not? Sometimes I find myself wishing that there was one simple answer to this complicated question.

First of all, there is a question of faith. One would think that the deeper the faith, the easier it would be to turn our lives over to God. But when Bill Wilson finally turned over his sobriety to God, it was as a last resort. At the time of his reaching out, he wasn't even sure if he really believed in God. Another person, who felt that God was using her to help others, told me, "It is entirely up to God, God's action and God's will. You just never know when and for whom God will intervene."

Try this and see if you agree. I think that we tend to turn to God when there is nothing else left to do. I remember when I tried to stop smoking, using all the various gimmicks. When all these "helps" failed, I turned to God . . . and this worked! When I realized, after quitting, that I never really wanted to go back, I said to God, "This has to be you. Until I turned to you as a last resort, I felt unsure. Now at last I am sure. Thank you." I thought I had this light in response to my prayer. I think God replied to me, "Oh, I could do other things in you and . through you more important than giving up smoking. But you have to experiment with your own formulae. When you find out that they are futile, and you are powerless, then you will come to me. You will turn to me with a complete surrender. Then I will be able to help you." Apparently, we have to "hit bottom" and to realize in some way that the only way we can go is "up." The way to do this, as the song says, is to keep our "hand in the hand of the Man."

What our own futile series of experiments prepares us for is a full-hearted surrender to God. Of course, God can do anything in us and for us. But somehow I think that normally we have to make a final and trusting commitment of our problem to God. If we think and worry about it, it seems to be a sure sign that we have not yet turned it over to God completely. Do you remember this anonymous verse?

Broken Dreams

As children bring their broken dreams
With tears for us to mend,
I brought my broken dreams to God
Because God is my friend.

But then, instead of leaving God
In peace to work alone,
I stayed around and tried to help
With ways that were my own.

At last I snatched them back
And cried, "How can you be so slow?"
"My child," God said, "what could I do?
You never did let go."

One more thought: Many times we like to speak to God in a way that we think is befitting. So we tell God nice things: "Oh, Heavenly Father, I am filled with the sweetest sentiments of faith, hope and charity." The real fact is that we are filled with homicidal urges. We wear a practiced mask when we are speaking to God. We think of it as rèspect, but it is in fact dishonesty. And not even God can communicate with a mask. A mask is a barrier that even God cannot penetrate without confirming us in our dishonesty.

So, it must be a complete and final surrender to the power of God, and it must be ourselves speaking in our own way. Then can we find the peace, power and presence that can be ours only in surrender.

One more thing: Enough *why* can endure almost any *how*. Translated it means that if one has enough motivation, that person can endure almost anything. Burnout, it has been said, is not the result of too much or too hard work. It is rather the indication of an increasing sense of futility. When the well runs dry, none of us feels moved to any kind of action. It is therefore important to keep ourselves motivated. How? I would suggest that we do the difficult thing for a special intention, for ourselves or for another. We might make a list of all the things that would be changed for ourselves and others if the intention is granted. This will keep us motivated, and we must remember: Enough *why* can endure any *how* that we might be going through. There really is no such thing as a strong or weak will, but only strong or weak motivation.

QUESTIONS FOR REFLECTION

1. What questions is life asking of me at this point in the course of my life?
2. What is my habit of ownership? Do I habitually take all the blame when things go wrong, or do I assign blame to someone or something else?
3. Is there anything in my past life about which I was once worried, but which I am now able to let go?
4. In my own experience, what has been the result of talking things over with an honest, nonjudgmental friend?
5. Is self-discovery really a lifelong process? What do I know about myself today that I didn't know five years ago? In the twilight of my life, what might I know about myself that I don't know now?

6. What is the hardest emotion for me to share? Is this difficult for me to share because of a value-conflict, parent tapes, peer pressure, or what?

7. What had you once seen as a problem that, once presented to another person, seemed like nothing at all?

8. What are your own thoughts and feelings about using "reevaluation counseling" as described above?

9. In what ways does the "God-box" seem like a challenge or a cop-out to you?

10. How do people turn something over to God completely, and still try to do their part?

11. Is there such a thing as a "strong" or "weak" will, or is it just that there is sufficient or lack of sufficient motivation?

12. Why is it so difficult to make a full-hearted and final surrender to God? Do our emotions always follow in line docilely?

13. What mask am I tempted to wear when speaking to God? Am I overly dependent or underdependent on God? What script do I use to sound appropriate to God?

14. Why do some people have "spiritual experiences" intensely and often, while others never seem to have them?

15. What is the hard part for me about putting "insights" to work in my day-to-day behavior?

ALSO BY JOHN POWELL

A Life-Giving Vision

Why Am I Afraid to Tell You Who I Am?

The Secret of Staying in Love

Why Am I Afraid to Love?

Fully Human, Fully Alive

He Touched Me

Unconditional Love

Reason to Live! Reason to Die!

Will the Real Me Please Stand Up?

Through Seasons of the Heart

Happiness Is an Inside Job